Dear Mrs. President

By Ana Maria Medici   •   Illustrated by Nurit Benchetrit Motchan

For Naya, and all those boldly living their dreams.

Dear Mrs. President

© 2021 Ana Maria Medici

Dear Mrs. President,

I believe you to be a brave woman.

Intelligent,

hardworking,

and compassionate.

When I see the things you do, I feel inspired.

You strive to help others, and work at making things more fair.

You have a family, but being a mother and wife does not solely define who you are. You reach further, helping our country, and the world.

I do not care about the style of your hair or what size dress you wear. I only insist that you be your most authentic self.

Your passion and your service are why
I write to you today.

I thank you for the leadership you give to our country, and the way you see each day as an opportunity to serve.

I thank you for teaching me that I, too,
can be anything I choose

Sincerely,
Naya Mendoza

PS, and very important:

Why are there only men on dollar bills?
I think you need to be the first female face
on American money (but definitely not the last).